Simple Solutions

Grooming

By Elizabeth Moyer
Illustrations by Jean Abernethy

With practical care tips

BOWTIE
PRESS®

A Division of BowTie, Inc.
Irvine, California

Karla Austin, *Business Operations Manager*
Nick Clemente, *Special Consultant*
Barbara Kimmel, *Managing Editor*
Jessica Knott, *Production Supervisor*
Amy Stirnkorb, *Designer*

The horses in this book are referred to as *she* and *he* in alternating chapters unless their sexes are apparent from the activities discussed.

Library of Congress Cataloging-in-Publication Data

Moyer, Elizabeth.
  Grooming / by Elizabeth Moyer ; illustrations by Jean Abernethy.
    p. cm. — (Horse illustrated simple solutions)
  ISBN-13: 978-1-931993-97-5
  ISBN-10: 1-931993-97-1
  1. Horses—Grooming. I. Title.

  SF285.7.M69 2007
  636.1'0833—dc22

                        2006038890

BowTie Press®
A Division of BowTie, Inc.
3 Burroughs
Irvine, California 92618

Printed and bound in Singapore
16 15 14 13 12 11 10 09 08 07   1 2 3 4 5 6 7 8 9 10

CONTENTS

The Benefits of Grooming

Daily grooming is an essential part of horse care. It's a simple process with many benefits and one of the first basic horsemanship skills to master. Most horses find grooming relaxing and enjoyable; in fact, many horse owners do, too! In addition to making your horse look nice, regular grooming benefits your horse's health and well-being. This beauty treatment is more than skin deep!

Grooming for Health

Grooming promotes circulation, stimulates the skin, and massages the muscles. It brings out the shine in your horse's coat by

loosening dead hair, bringing up dirt and dandruff (scurf), and distributing the natural oils.

By grooming regularly, you can keep tabs on your horse's weight and health. You'll become familiar with the landscape of her body and know what is normal for her—and notice when something is amiss. As you groom, inspect your horse for cuts, skin irritations, unusual swellings, areas of pain or sensitivity, and anything else out of the ordinary. Horses groomed regularly stay healthier because someone is keeping a close eye on them to detect problems sooner rather than later. Although grooming adds polish, your horse's shiny coat truly begins within. Good nutrition and regular health care are essential to keeping your horse looking and feeling her best.

Grooming for a Good Relationship

By providing hands-on time, grooming builds a relationship between you and your horse and helps strengthen your bond. Among horses, mutual grooming—scratching with the teeth, nibbling, and so on—is a friendly way they relate and show affection. Your grooming activities often mean the same thing to horses. Through this routine interaction, you will develop a feel for your horse's general temperament, come to understand her quirks, and learn how to handle her effectively. In turn, she will learn where you stand in the hierarchy: grooming offers an opportunity to reinforce your leadership role and your horse's respect for you.

The grooming process is a good way to get acquainted with a new horse. Even with a familiar horse, a preride grooming session

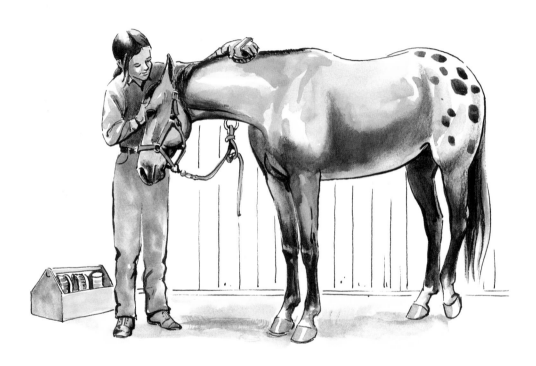

lets you assess how your mount is feeling that day, giving you clues as to what may be in store once you get in the saddle. Is she relaxed? Grumpy? Nervous?

Grooming is a great get-to-know-you and get-to-know-you-better activity for both horse and human. By investing some time and using some elbow grease, you'll be well acquainted with your horse on all levels and be able to take pride in her well-kept appearance.

Brushes and Tools

Your grooming kit can be strictly functional or, if you really enjoy pampering your horse, filled with the newest types of colorful, specialized, ergonomically designed brushes and tools. For hygienic reasons, it's best if each horse has an exclusive set of brushes and grooming tools because fungus can spread through shared grooming equipment. Brushes and grooming tools should be cleaned periodically. When necessary, soak them in diluted bleach, mild detergent or shampoo, and lay them out to dry.

Brushes come in a variety of textures and with either natural or synthetic bristles. Soft brushes and gentler tools can be used on the bony, sensitive areas of horses' bodies; stiff brushes can tackle

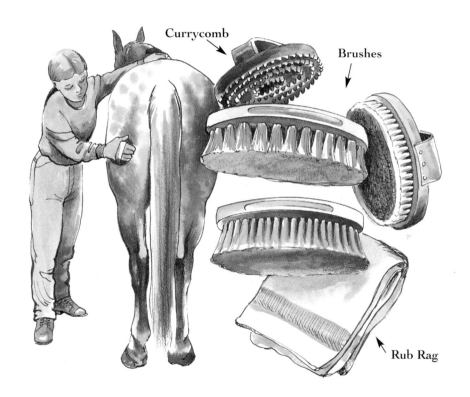

Currycomb

Brushes

Rub Rag

brawny regions and tough hides. Be attentive to your horse's reactions, and pick the type of brush that seems most comfortable to him. If he's thin-skinned and sensitive, stiff, sharp bristles are tortuous and soft bristles more tolerable. If he's a tough, itchy guy with a yaklike coat, however, he may love the strongest brush you've got.

Here are the basic brushes and tools you will need for your grooming kit:

Currycomb—Used in a circular motion, the currycomb removes loose hair and brings dander and dirt to the surface, where they can be brushed off. Currying also provides a mini-massage for your horse. Currycombs come in a variety of shapes and strengths. The most popular types are made of rubber and have rows of raised teeth, fingers, or textured nubs. Soft, flexible styles with small nubs are gentle and can be used even on such sensitive areas as faces, flanks, bellies, and legs; firmer currycombs are better for thick coats and tough dirt, such as dried mud. Sharp-toothed metal currycombs should not be used on a horse, but they can come in handy for cleaning the bristles of your brushes.

Stiff brush—Often referred to as a dandy brush, this workhorse of a brush has stiff bristles to tackle tough dirt and dried mud and sweat on the horse's body. Avoid using this brush on sensitive areas such as the face and the legs.

Soft brushes—Use a soft brush to bring up the shine and remove the dust from the coat. A body brush designed with short,

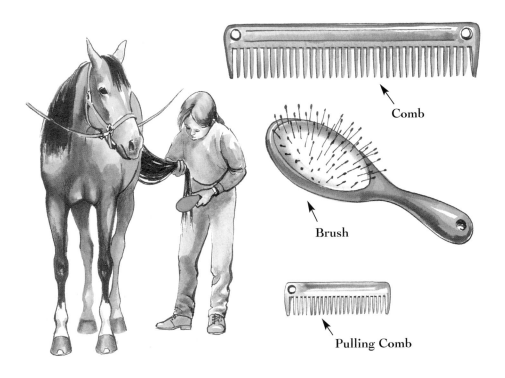

Comb

Brush

Pulling Comb

soft bristles deep cleans and distributes oils throughout the coat for a natural shine. A soft finishing brush has long bristles to flick off surface dust. Your grooming routine can incorporate either or both of these soft brushes.

Brush and comb for mane and tail—For mane and tail care, use any or all of the following: a wide-tooth plastic comb; a hairbrush (vented or paddle-style pin brushes work well); and a small metal pulling comb if you plan to pull, or shorten, your horse's mane. The metal pulling comb is not recommended for any purpose other than pulling, as it tends to break hairs easily.

Hoof pick—A hoof pick is one of a horse person's most essential tools. It is used for the vital task of removing stones, manure, and dirt from hooves. Choose a simple metal design or a plastic-handle style that incorporates a stiff brush on the opposite side of the pick.

In addition to the basics listed above, your grooming kit should include the following items:

Sponge(s) — A large sponge is ideal for using on the body; a smaller sponge works well for washing the face. Many people designate separate sponges for specific areas, such as the eyes, the nostrils, and the dock area under the tail.

Towels or soft cloths — "Rub rags" are invaluable for many grooming chores, such as cleaning the face, spot cleaning, polishing the coat, or toweling off after a bath.

Sweat scraper — After a bath, the sweat scraper removes excess water from your horse's coat. Sweat scrapers are typically made

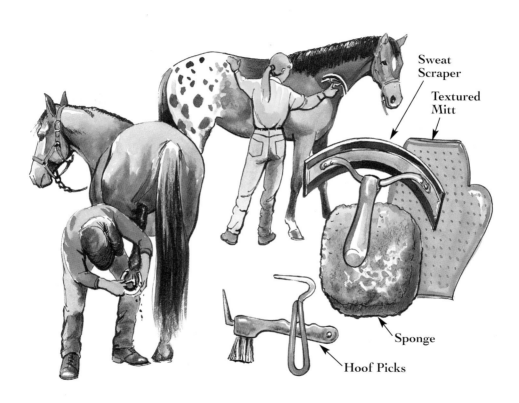

Sweat Scraper

Textured Mitt

Sponge

Hoof Picks

of plastic or lightweight metal. Some equine "squeegees" are designed with a flexible rubber edge to follow the contours of the horse's body. A multitasking sweat scraper made of folding flexible metal features a flat sweat scraper on one side and teeth for use as a shedding blade on the other.

Storage tote, bucket, or carryall — Stash your grooming gear in a handy, portable container.

Here are some extra items you may want to include in your grooming kit:

Grooming mitts — These handy helpers perform a variety of grooming functions. Pebbled or textured mitts can be used for bathing and currying; soft fleece mitts polish the coat to a high sheen and make good applicators for fly spray or coat polish.

Detangler—Mane and tail detanglers (gel or spray) help remove knots in the mane and the tail to make brushing easier. They often include moisturizing ingredients for conditioning as well.

Coat polish—Coat-polish sprays are meant for occasional use to add shine. These products also repel dust, which helps cut down on grooming time. They help keep manes and tails tangle free as well. Coat-polish sprays are slick, so avoid using them in the saddle area.

Shedding block—When brushed across your horse's coat, this rough, porous stone picks up loose hair during shedding season and also removes botfly eggs (undesirable parasite larvae that appear as small yellow dots on your horse's legs).

Fly repellent — Fly spray can be applied while you are grooming and caring for your horse's coat. Thorough application will help keep your horse free from flying pests during fly season. Some fly sprays contain conditioners and sunscreen to protect the coat. Others are designed to provide long-lasting protection. Roll-on formulas can be applied to the face.

Shampoo — It's important to use a shampoo formulated for horses. Avoid harsh detergents, which can dull and dry the coat. There are some shampoos made specifically for whitening and stain removal. Conditioners for equine coats are also available in leave-in or rinse-out formulas.

Spray-on spot remover — When a bath isn't practical, quickly remove stains from your horse's coat with spray-on spot removers.

Hoof dressing — Hoof dressing is designed to condition the feet. Dry, brittle, cracked feet may benefit from a moisturizing conditioner. Follow product directions regarding application. It's always a good idea to consult your farrier or veterinarian about the condition of your horse's hooves to determine the most appropriate product for your horse as well as to identify and address any underlying hoof concerns.

Clippers — For cutting-edge beauty, clippers are handy to have in your grooming kit. A small- or medium-size model should be able to handle the most basic clipping tasks, such as trimming faces and legs.

The Grooming Process

Horses are creatures of habit and take great comfort in routine. Having a consistent daily grooming procedure adds to their sense of security. Over time, you'll develop a grooming routine that optimizes your efficiency and your horse's comfort. Work with your horse's preferences so that grooming is as enjoyable—or as tolerable—as possible.

Basic grooming involves a set of everyday steps. There are additional grooming procedures that need to be carried out periodically for health and maintenance or on a seasonal basis.

Steps to Good Grooming

Grooming before riding is a must because the heat and friction created by tack on a dirty horse can cause sores and irritation. It makes sense to groom from top to bottom and front to back so that you remove dirt in a logical, systematic manner and are not dirtying what you've just brushed. It's also more efficient to groom one side of the horse, then to move to the other. Another rule of thumb is to start with the stiffest brush or tool and to finish with the softest. When grooming, your goal is to loosen and remove dirt first, then to smooth the coat and polish it to a nice shine.

Before you begin, your horse should be haltered and tied—you can't groom a moving target. Be sure to tie your horse safely using a quick-release knot or by cross tying with panic snaps.

Picking out your horse's hooves is the most important grooming chore, so make this the first task on your list. Before you lift your horse's hoof, run your bare hand down her leg, feeling for heat or swelling. This small step could detect a potentially debilitating leg injury in its early stages.

To pick out your horse's hooves, stand parallel to one of the horse's legs, facing toward her tail. Run the hand nearest the horse down the back of the leg to just above the fetlock joint, and

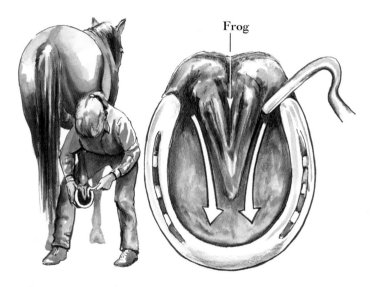

Frog

give a gentle squeeze. This should prompt most horses to lift the foot. If it doesn't, squeeze a little harder. After the horse lifts her hoof, support it with one hand, and pick it out with a hoof pick held in the other hand. Working from heel to toe, remove packed mud and manure, and clean the V-shaped grooves around the frog portion. The frog is a sensitive area so be careful not to dig into it with your pick. A built-in brush on the hoof pick is handy for sweeping away any remaining dirt on the sole. Set the hoof down gently when you are done.

It makes sense to start grooming your horse's body at the top. Brush the mane first so any dust and debris that shakes out onto the coat will be removed as you continue grooming.

Next, you can tackle the largest area to be groomed—the coat. Start working on the coat using a currycomb. Begin at the neck and shoulder, and work your way down the body and toward the tail. Using small circular motions, curry as vigorously as

Upward flick removes dirt

Cross Ties

Swipe the brush across
the currycomb to clean it.

your horse will tolerate for the maximum massaging action and dirt removal. Periodically tap out the hair and dirt that builds up in the currycomb.

Follow by using the stiff

brush on your horse's body to remove the hair and the dirt that the currycomb has loosened. Use firm strokes to brush in the direction of hair growth, and add an upward flick of the wrist to lift the dirt. Follow with a soft brush to remove any remaining fine particles of dirt, dander, and surface dust from the body. Use your soft brush on the face and legs as well.

Put some power behind your cleaning. Firm strokes are more effective than tentative swipes, which can also be ticklish and annoying to some horses. Your horse will let you know if you are brushing too hard by moving away, pinning her ears, or exhibiting other negative reactions.

For the most efficient coat cleaning, keep your currycomb in one hand and your brush in the other. Swipe the bristles of your brush across the currycomb every few strokes to clean the brush so you are not redepositing dirt on the coat. Another time-saving grooming technique is to use a brush in each hand, stroking one after the other and periodically whisking the brushes together to clean the bristles.

The last area to groom is the tail. Use your fingers to remove shavings and hay from the tail. Smooth it down so that it hangs nicely. A tail that is routinely detangled and cared for should be easy to maintain without too much daily work. Because tail hair can be fragile, whether or not to brush the tail every day is a point of debate among horse people. You'll need to determine which approach works best to keep your horse's tail in top condition: daily care or periodic maintenance.

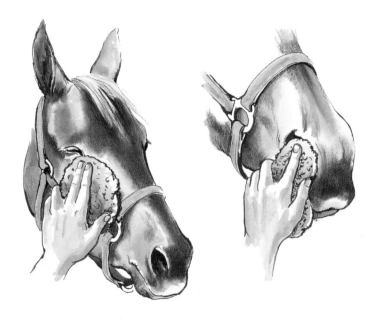

For the finishing touches, sponge away discharge from the eyes and the nostrils. If you are being thorough, clean under the tail and between the hindquarters.

Finish with a rubdown using a towel, a soft cloth, or a fleece grooming mitt to pick up any remaining dust on your horse's body and to polish the coat.

Grooming after riding is also essential. It's considered poor horsemanship to put your horse away with sweat marks. Worse, dried sweat left in the coat is itchy and uncomfortable and may cause your horse to develop skin problems. Rinse off sweat and mud (weather permitting), or let it dry and immediately brush it out.

Even when you are not riding, daily grooming is ideal. If pressed for time, you can abbreviate your routine to the most essential chores, such as picking out the feet. Be sure to perform a thorough grooming the next time you care for your horse. Then, on a weekly or monthly basis, tackle additional jobs such as bathing, clipping, or mane pulling to keep your horse looking her best. Think of it as a horsey spa day!

Grooming for Good Hygiene

In addition to the routine grooming steps that keep your horse looking good, there are cleaning tasks that should be done periodically for health and hygiene. Your male horse will eventually need his sheath cleaned. The sheath is a pouchlike structure surrounding the penis where dirt, dead skin, and oily secretions combine and build up inside. Most horses require cleaning only once or twice a year, but some need more frequent attention. You may notice your horse's sheath is swollen or detect an odor or black gunk around the area when he is in need of cleaning.

Some horses allow you to safely accomplish this task; others have to be sedated by a veterinarian. If your horse is difficult about having this area of his body approached, it is best to let your veterinarian handle the chore.

To clean the sheath, wash inside and out using warm water and either a commercial sheath-cleaning product or mild soap, such as Ivory. Rubber gloves are recommended for the job. You can use roll cotton or a small sponge to help remove the chunks of debris. It is also important to completely rinse the soap or cleanser because soap residue can irritate this sensitive area.

When cleaning the sheath, do not bend or squat down underneath the horse where you could easily get kicked. Reach deep inside the folds of the sheath. The job is easier if your horse will relax and drop his penis to be cleaned as well. Don't overlook the pocket at the tip of the penis where debris can form into a hard ball, or bean, which needs to be removed so it doesn't interfere with urination. Removing the bean is a touchy process that may require your veterinarian's assistance.

Mares get a similar buildup between their teats and need to have the udder area cleaned on a regular basis.

Seasonal Grooming Concerns

In winter, a horse's coat can resemble a woolly mammoth's. This cozy coat loses its insulating properties if it becomes soaked or matted down. After riding or if your horse gets wet, dry the coat thoroughly, and fluff it up to prevent her from becoming chilled. Winter grooming helps detect problems that may be hidden under a thick coat. If your horse is blanketed, regular grooming, along with keeping blankets clean, prevents skin irritations from developing.

In spring and fall, you'll have to contend with shedding. As you roll up your sleeves and begin currying to assist the shedding process, prepare for hair flying everywhere. Get out your shedding block to help, too.

In summer, add fly spray to your grooming routine. Lightly spray the fly repellent on the coat until it is slightly damp. A technique to thoroughly coat the hair shaft with repellent is to brush against the hair growth, apply the spray, then brush with the hair growth, and spray again. Use a towel or mitt to apply fly spray to the face.

Keep in mind that wet, muddy, or humid conditions often cause fungal or bacterial skin problems that need treatment. Ticks are also a hazard in some regions. Look for them burrowing into the skin, especially around your horse's mane and tail. Use tweezers to carefully remove each tick. To ensure you remove the entire tick, grasp it as close to the skin of the horse as possible, and pull away using a steady motion. Disinfect the area afterward.

Hoof Care

Hooves are prone to many injuries and maladies that attentive grooming can often detect or prevent. For example, a stone wedged in your horse's hoof can cause painful bruising. Or, your horse may step on a nail or other sharp object and injure the bottom of his foot. Additionally, hooves that are not cleaned on a regular basis are prone to infection. To prevent injuries and infections, pick out your horse's feet every day as well as before and after riding.

As you pick out your horse's feet, pay attention to their condition. A moist, foul-smelling black discharge indicates that your horse has thrush, a hoof infection often caused by unsanitary

conditions. Thrush can usually be treated effectively with one of the many topical remedies available at tack and feed supply stores; however, if left untreated, thrush can cause lameness.

In addition, examine the horseshoes and nails, checking that they are firmly in place. Finally, keep an eye on hoof growth, and maintain a regular schedule of farrier care; most horses need their hooves trimmed every six to eight weeks. Maintaining proper moisture balance in the hooves can be an issue. Ask your farrier about the condition of your horse's hooves and whether he or she recommends using a hoof dressing. Regular farrier care, along with daily maintenance, will keep your horse's feet healthy.

Mane and Tail Care

Your horse's mane and tail can be crowning glories or tangled nightmares. But a little regular maintenance will keep these tresses tamed.

Your horse's hairstyle may be related to the tradition of her breed or the type of riding you do. For some breeds (Andalusians, Arabians, and Morgans, to name a few) and in certain riding sports (reining, for example), the mane is typically left long and flowing. Many horses, however, wear short manes to create a tidy look.

Everyone loves a long, full tail. Some horses are endowed with more tail hair than others; careful grooming helps any tail stay in its best condition.

Long Manes

If your horse has a long mane, your grooming goal is to keep dreadlocks from forming. One technique for controlling an extremely luxuriant mane is to braid it. A number of big loose braids will keep the mane clean and tangle free. Be sure not to pull too tightly at the roots; a tight braid may make your horse

itch, causing her to rub her mane, which results in unsightly breakage. Comb and rebraid the mane at least once a week.

Some horses have thick unruly manes that lie on both sides of the neck. To train the mane to stay to one side, dampen the hair, comb it to one side, and braid it down. You can add styling gel to encourage it to stay put.

Short Manes

Shortening the mane is accomplished by a technique called pulling, which thins and shortens the hair to a uniform length and thickness and leaves unevenly layered, natural-looking ends. Never cut the mane straight across with scissors—this leaves an obvious and awkward-looking blunt edge.

To pull a mane, separate a small section of hair up to ½-inch thick. Grasp the hairs at their ends, and comb back toward the roots using a small metal pulling comb. After backcombing the section, you'll be left holding only the longest hairs from the bunch. Wrap these hairs around the pulling comb, and give a firm tug to remove the hair at the roots. The roots of the mane hair are fairly insensitive compared with our roots, so pulling generally doesn't hurt the horse.

Continue pulling small sections of hair along the neck to achieve an even length. A good length for a pulled mane is 4 inches. Pull conservatively at first; you can always go back and make it shorter.

There are special pulling combs that are designed to make the job easier by razoring off the hair with a built-in blade. These

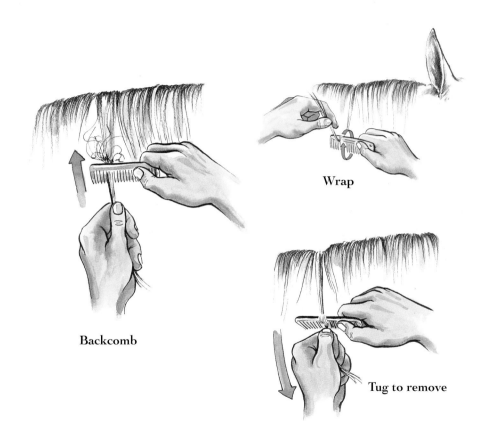

Backcomb

Wrap

Tug to remove

combs also leave the desired irregular edge for a more natural look.

For horses with extremely sparse manes, shortening the mane without thinning it too much can be a challenge. In these cases, use scissors, held vertically, to snip off the length without sacrificing fullness.

If your horse objects to mane pulling, there are several tactics you can employ to make the process more bearable for her:

- Pull fewer hairs at a time.
- Pull a small section of hair every day rather than pulling the entire mane in one session. Using this technique, your horse may even become better about the chore over time.
- Pull the mane after exercise. Because the horse's pores are open, the hair will come out more easily.

Tails

There are two schools of thought on the proper handling of a horse's tail. Some horse people believe in handling the tail as little as possible to minimize hair breakage and loss. Others believe that routine primping, braiding, and bagging the tail pro-tects the hair and keeps tangles from getting out of control. Regardless of the theory you embrace, always handle the tail hair with care.

To groom a horse's tail, first run your fingers through it. A detangling product will make the job easier. Work through knots patiently by hand. Once you can run your fingers through the tail, follow with a brush, starting at the bottom and working up.

Some horse owners like to keep the tail in a single thick braid to prevent tangles from forming. Start with a clean, conditioned tail, and braid below the tailbone. You can also encase the plaited tail in a protective tail bag, which attaches below the tailbone. (Never wrap anything around the tailbone

Braid

that could compromise blood circulation.) If you braid and bag the tail, be sure to take it down and redo it weekly.

Besides tangles, tail rubbing is a common grooming challenge. This habit breaks hairs at the top of the tail and often leaves an unsightly bald spot. Tail rubbing may also signify a health-care concern, such as parasite infestation, and it can indicate a dirty sheath or udder. Because horses can't reach these areas to scratch, tail rubbing is the closest they can come. Product buildup at the tail head can also cause itching.

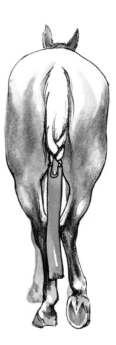

Tail Bag

Bathing

For everyday purposes, a quick hose down or sponge bath works well to remove sweat and grime. However, an occasional shampoo will leave your horse sparkling clean.

Pick a warm day that's not too breezy to bathe your horse, and take all your supplies to the wash rack or bathing area. Along with access to a water supply, the bathing area should have good drainage, nonslip footing, and a safe place to tie your horse.

Here is a list of supplies you should gather:

• **Bucket**

• **Equine Shampoo** — This shampoo is pH balanced for equine skin and coats. It's best to use products formulated for horses.

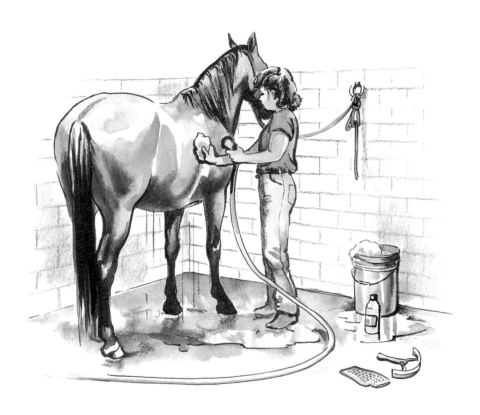

- **Sponge**

- **Sweat scraper**

Optional items include:

- **Equine conditioner** — A conditioner made for horses is great for the mane and the tail and will keep the coat soft and shiny.

- **Grooming mitt** — A textured mitt lifts deeply embedded dirt.

- **Adjustable spray nozzle** — A nozzle helps conserve water, and some sensitive horses prefer the gentle shower or mist settings.

- **Warm water** — Not every barn has the luxury of running hot water. If there isn't any, you can make bathing more pleasant for your horse by heating a few buckets of water with a heater coil (don't leave unattended!) or solar power (leave the buckets in the sun to warm up for a few hours).

To begin bathing your horse, prepare some suds in a bucket. Squirt the shampoo in first, then add water. This dilute mixture allows you to apply the shampoo evenly to your horse's body and is easier to rinse from the coat.

Thoroughly wet your horse's coat with plain water, taking care around his head. Some horses will tolerate having their faces sprayed with a hose, but others won't, so you may need to use a sponge to wet the face instead.

Once your horse is wet, dip into your suds and lather up your horse's body, then move on to the mane and tail. You can use full-strength shampoo on the mane and the top of the tail; scrub deeply at the roots where dirt and scurf lurk. Dunk the length of the tail in a bucket of suds. Shampoo the head only if absolutely necessary; it can be difficult to rinse the shampoo out, and you don't want to get it in your horse's eyes or nose.

Because soap residue is itchy and it dries and dulls the coat, it's crucial to completely rinse out the shampoo. To make sure you get out all of the shampoo, continue rinsing until you don't see any bubbles and the coat is squeaky clean; then rinse some more! If you're using conditioner, follow the manufacturer's directions—some are designed to be left in, whereas others should be rinsed out.

After your final rinse, use the sweat scraper to squeegee excess water from your horse's coat to help it dry faster. Tie or hand graze your horse in a sunny area so he can dry before you put him away. Horses often like to follow your scrub with their idea of good grooming: a nice roll in the dirt!

A Little Trim

A little attention to detail with the clippers puts the finishing touches on a well-groomed appearance. Show horses have every last whisker and extraneous hair removed to create an ultra-sleek look. Although such extensive clipping is not necessary for a casual everyday lifestyle, some simple trimming around the ears, jawline, and fetlocks makes your horse look neat and tidy. Before clipping, consider your horse's living conditions. Some of these shaggy hairs serve a purpose for horses that live outside, such as providing warmth in winter or protection from pesky flies.

For these little tidying jobs, small- or medium-size clippers are quiet, lightweight, and easily maneuverable. The cordless,

Before
After

rechargeable kinds are especially handy. Clipper blades come in different sizes: the higher the number, the closer the shave. A #10 blade is useful for most purposes and is relatively forgiving of any mistakes.

Make sure your horse accepts the noise and vibration of the clippers before you clip her. If your horse is afraid of the clippers or has never been exposed to them, don't force the issue. Take the time necessary to introduce her to the clippers, and let her become accustomed to their sound and feel before you take on any clipping task.

Skimming the "beard" under your horse's jawline with the clippers creates a more refined profile. Using a light touch, remove the long shaggy hairs, working in the direction of hair growth. However, for the groove under the chin, you will have to turn the clippers around to get at the long hairs.

Trimming the longest inner ear hairs will leave your horse looking sleek while still providing some protection. To clip your

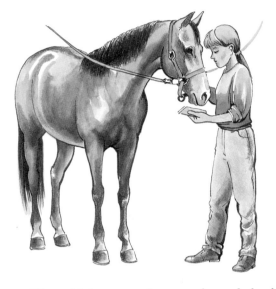

horse's ears, gently bring the edges of the ears together, then trim the protruding tufts of hair. Next, lightly run your clippers around the edges of the ears to tidy them.

The whiskers on the muzzle and the long guard hairs around the eyes are sometimes trimmed. However, these hairs serve an important purpose: to help a horse sense his surroundings and avoid potential injuries to his eyes or face. It's best to leave these

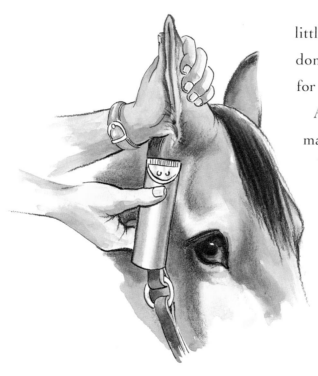

little feeler hairs if they don't need to be removed for the show ring.

A small section of the mane behind the ears can be trimmed to create a bridle path, or place for the crownpiece of the bridle to rest comfortably. As a rule of thumb, use the width of the crownpiece to guide

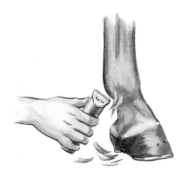 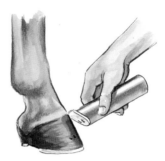

how much hair to trim. Be careful not to take off too much; a bad haircut in this area can take months to grow out.

You can tidy the look of your horse's legs by clipping the shaggy hair from the fetlocks and legs. To clip these areas, lightly run your clippers down the lower leg in the direction of hair growth. You may have to maneuver the clippers a bit to get underneath the fetlock joint. Finish by edging the hairline above

the hoof around the coronary band.

Grooming doesn't have to be just another dirty job. It can be quality time you spend with your horse that also yields visible results. You'll enjoy the satisfaction of seeing your efforts shining in front of you in the form of a well-kept horse.

About the Author

Elizabeth Moyer is the editor of *Horse Illustrated* magazine, an award-winning title and one of the nation's largest equine publications. She has been with the magazine since 1999. Prior to that, she worked in advertising. She is a horse owner and lifelong equestrian. Grooming has always been one of her favorite parts of equestrian life because there are few horsey things more satisfying than an equine makeover. She has sat in almost every type of saddle but is currently pursuing her interest in dressage. Her horse Teddy, a Dutch Warmblood, is the lucky recipient of many simple solutions grooming techniques.